THE CIVIL WAR:
America Torn Apart (1860-1865)

TITLE LIST

THE CIVIL WAR:
America Torn Apart (1860-1865)

BY WESLEY WINDSOR

MASON CREST

Mason Crest
370 Reed Road
Broomall, Pennsylvania 19008
www.masoncrest.com

Printed and bound in Hashemite Kingdom of Jordan.

First printing
9 8 7 6 5 4 3 2 1

Library of Congress Cataloging-in-Publication Data

Windsor, Wesley.
  The Civil War : America torn apart, 1860-1865 / by Wesley Windsor.
    p. cm. — (How America became America)
  ISBN 978-1-4222-2404-5 (hardcover) — ISBN 978-1-4222-2396-3 (series hardcover)
ISBN 978-1-4222-9314-0 (ebook)
 1. United States—History—Civil War, 1861-1865—Juvenile literature. I. Title.
 E468.W75 2012
 973.7—dc22
                                    2011001860

Produced by Harding House Publishing Services, Inc.
www.hardinghousepages.com
Cover design by Torque Advertising + Design.

1619—A Dutch ship trades twenty Africans to the Jamestown settlers. These first Africans are treated more like servants than slaves.

1850—The Compromise of 1850. It tries to make both the North and the South happy. Part of the law is the Fugitive Slave Act.

1858—Abraham Lincoln runs against Stephen Douglas in the Illinois Senate race. They argue about the expansion of slavery. Lincoln is against it and Douglas is for it. Douglas wins the election.

1856—People who want slavery and people who don't want slavery move to Kansas to vote. They start fighting with each other.

1793—Eli Whitney creates the cotton gin.

1820—The Missouri Compromise is passed. No slave states are allowed to be created north of Missouri's southern border.

May 1856—Senator Charles Sumner gives a speech against slavery. Two days later, a senator from South Carolina attacks him in Congress. People in the North are angry. People in the South are happy that someone finally stood up to the North.

1860—South Carolina is unhappy that Lincoln is President. South Carolina drops out of the United States. Next to drop out are Mississippi, Florida, Alabama, Georgia, Louisiana and Texas.

1846–1848—The Mexican War is fought over Texas.

1861—The Southern states form the Confederate States of America. The Confederate Army attacks Fort Sumter in South Carolina. The head of the troops at Fort Sumter knows he can't win. He gives up the fort to South Carolina. This is the first battle of the Civil War.

July 1–3, 1863—The Battle of Gettysburg. It is one of the biggest battles ever fought. The North wins the battle. From here on, things go better for the North.

April 14, 1865—President Abraham Lincoln is killed. John Wilkes Booth shoots him during a play at Ford's Theater. Lincoln dies the next morning.

November 1863—President Lincoln makes a famous speech at the Soldiers' National Cemetery in Gettysburg.

March 2, 1867—Congress passes the Reconstruction Act. Southern state governments are broken up. Northern troops are left in the South to keep control of it.

Autumn 1864—Union General William T. Sherman's March to the Sea. Sherman burns houses and entire cities on his way through Georgia. He reaches Savannah in December. He writes to President Lincoln offering him the city as a Christmas gift.

April 9, 1865—Confederate General Robert E. Lee surrenders to Union General Ulysses S. Grant. Lee's surrender ends the Civil War.

September 22, 1862—Lincoln makes the Emancipation Proclamation. It says that all slaves are free. It makes the war more about ending slavery.

1876—The presidential election doesn't produce a winner. Both the Republicans and the Democrats think that they won. After some arguing, the Republicans win. The new president is Rutherford B. Hayes.

Slave houses on a plantation.

Chapter One
SLAVERY

The first slaves came to the American colonies in 1619. A Dutch ship traded twenty Africans for food at Jamestown. This meant slavery began only twelve years after the colony began.

These first Africans were considered a type of servant. They could earn their freedom. As the years went by, though, this changed. Soon, Africans were sold as slaves in the Americas. And these slaves did not have any way to become free.

Buying slaves was cheaper than paying workers. So Americans told themselves it was okay to own other people. They said black people weren't as good as white people. They even said blacks weren't really human. They said the Africans were better off in North America, too. These things weren't true. People used these arguments to make themselves believe slavery was okay.

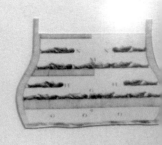

African people were brought to the New World under extreme conditions, then forced to live as slaves.

At first, Americans mostly used slaves to work on tobacco farms. Tobacco was hard on the soil, though. It used up the soil quickly. Once that happened, the land was no longer good to grow crops. Farmers had to keep finding new land for their tobacco fields. This got expensive. Also, people in Britain stopped buying as much tobacco.

The number of slaves had grown a lot, too. Children had been born to the Africans. Some slave owners had more slaves than they had work for them to do. The owners had to make sure the slaves had food, clothes, and a place to sleep. That cost a lot of money. Some people started to think it would be best to free their slaves.

Then, in 1793, Eli Whitney invented the cotton gin. The cotton gin was a machine that took the seeds out of cotton. Before this, the seeds had to be taken out by hand. This took a very long time. Not many people grew cotton, since it was so hard to clean out the seeds.

The cotton gin, though, made it easy. Suddenly, everyone wanted to grow cotton. Slave owners stopped thinking about freeing their slaves. Instead, they built huge cotton farms called plantations. The slaves worked on the cotton plantations.

Some people got very rich growing cotton. They built big houses and owned hundreds of slaves. These are the slave owners people usually think of today. Not all slave owners were rich, though. A lot of them were ordinary working people. Most slave owners owned only a few slaves.

Only the poorest white people in the South didn't own slaves. But even these people usually said slavery was a good thing. This might have been partly because they hoped that someday they would get rich. Then they would be able to own slaves themselves.

Sometimes, people did free their slaves. They freed them as a reward for good service. Some people freed their slaves only if they were too old or sick to work. These slave owners weren't really being kind. If they freed slaves who couldn't work, the owners

Eli Whitney

didn't have to look after them anymore. These slaves then had to find some way to take care of themselves.

Freed slaves also had to deal with **racism**. Because almost all black people in the United States were slaves in the early 1800s, they couldn't blend in. If people saw a black person, they usually assumed he was a slave. Sometimes free black people were captured and sold again as slaves. People said they must have been runaway slaves. Or else whites just didn't care whether or not they were runaways.

Racism is the belief that people from a certain race (whether black, Asian, whites, or Native) aren't as good as other people.

STETSON'S
UNCLE TOM'S CABIN
BOOKED BY
KLAW & ERLANGER

As Americans moved into the Western territories, slave owners wanted to bring their slaves with them. People in the Northern states worried about this. In the North, slavery had been outlawed since around 1800. There were two main reasons why people in the North didn't like the idea of slavery spreading.

First, a lot of Northerners worried that slavery was evil. They believed it was wrong to make other people slaves. They had heard the stories from escaped slaves. They knew how bad life could be for slaves. A book called *Uncle Tom's Cabin*, by Harriet Beecher Stowe, told about slaves' lives. People who read it were horrified. They couldn't believe people were being treated that way.

The second reason some Northerners didn't want slavery to spread was that they worried that slaves would take their jobs. Then there wouldn't be enough work for white people. So they wanted to get rid of blacks. They wanted to send them away from the United States.

JOBS AND RACISM

As long as America has existed, Americans have worried that other groups will take away their jobs. This is one reason why many people from other countries have faced racism. It's easier to tell yourself it's okay not to welcome people to America if you believe those people are not as good as you are. And yet, America has always been a nation built by people from many different groups. All those different kinds of people have helped make America strong.

Today, America still struggles with this problem. In the twenty-first century, many Americans worry Hispanics coming to America will take away jobs from other Americans. They don't believe these people will help make the United States stronger. Instead, they fear Hispanics may make other Americans poorer.

What do you think? Is this situation at all like the way some Northerners felt about blacks during the 1800s? Why or why not?

Cotton gin being operated by slaves.

In 1822, the American Colonization Society started the country of Liberia in Africa. Liberia was supposed to be a country where people who had once been slaves could live. The society sent thousands of freed slaves to live in Liberia. The colony didn't work out very well, though. Most of the freed slaves had lived their whole lives in the United States. They thought of themselves as Americans. They weren't used to life in Africa. They had trouble fitting into Africa.

Some Americans had thought Liberia would be the perfect solution for the black people in the United States. They were disappointed it didn't work better.

By the middle of the 1800s, Americans were split over the issue of slavery. Soon, this would lead to a fight.

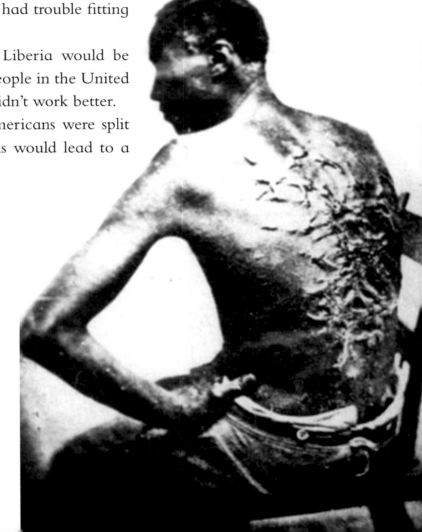

Scars left on an African American after he was whipped by his white "owners."

The Northern states needed the cotton that the South grew, and the South needed the North's factories to produce finished goods made from the cotton.

Chapter Two
NORTH AND SOUTH DIVIDED

Slavery was in the middle of the problems between the North and the South. But it wasn't the only problem.

The Northern states and the Southern states were very different from each other. The South had lots of farms. The North, on the other hand, had more factories. The North used the cotton grown in the South to make cloth. They also made a lot of money selling food and other things to people in the South.

Since the North had more jobs, most **immigrants** moved to those states. The population in the North grew much faster than in the South.

The people in the South weren't very happy with the North. People in the North didn't have slaves. They said slavery was wrong. But they didn't mind buying cotton grown by slaves. They didn't mind selling things to slave owners. All the buying and selling in the United States was mixed up with slavery. It was almost impossible to escape from it. Even people who believed slavery was wrong still wore clothes made from the cotton grown by slaves.

Immigrants are people who leave their homelands and move to another country to live.

WHAT WOULD YOU HAVE DONE?

Today we know how evil slavery was. It's easy to think if we'd been alive in the 1800s, we would have had no part in slavery. But it's very hard to step outside the world where you live. Today, for example, we know our clothing is often made in countries where the workers are treated very badly. Sometimes young children work in the factories where our clothing is made. These factories are often unsafe. We know this is wrong. And yet most of us don't stop buying and wearing clothes made this way!

It's hard to know what we should do to change things. And the people who lived in America in the 1800s faced the same kind of problem. It's hard to change something as big as slavery. It takes brave people who are willing to speak up for what's right. And it means that everybody has to be willing to change the way they live. Even if the answers are sometimes hard to find, that's never an excuse for not doing what's right!

But many people in the North believed slavery was wrong. Some of these Northerners helped slaves escape. People in the South considered this stealing.

The Underground Railroad was a network of Northerners who helped people escape slavery. The Underground Railroad wasn't a real railroad. It was a way to get people from the South to the North, though. It was built of barns and caves and secret rooms where people could rest and hide. These were called "stations." White people and free black people hid the escaping slaves. They helped move them secretly from place to place. They were sometimes called "conductors." Not all escaping slaves used the Underground Railroad. A lot of them didn't even know it existed. But over 100,000 slaves used the Underground Railroad to find freedom.

Abolitionists were people in the North who believed slavery should end

Underground Railroad monument.

forever. They said it was wrong to make other people slaves. Slave owners in the South were angry with the abolitionists.

In the first half of the 1800s, the number of slave and free states were nearly equal. That meant that neither side had more power than the other. More and more people in the North started arguing against slavery, though. People in the South worried the United States would keep slavery from spreading into the West. They worried there would soon be more free states than slave states. If that happened, free states might control Congress. That meant they would have more power. They would be able to make decisions about the slave states.

For quite a while, the United States kept the number of free and slave states balanced. When a new slave state joined the Union, a new free state would be added, too. That made sure there were always around the same number of each.

In 1820, Missouri joined the United States as a slave state. At the same time, Maine joined as a free state. Congress passed a law called the Missouri **Compromise**. The Missouri Compromise said that any new states north of Missouri's southern border would be free states.

The Mexican War, from 1846 to 1848, raised the question of slavery again. The United States suddenly had the chance to gain even more land. Both the slave states and free states wanted to claim the land for their side. Leaders from the North and those from the South had very different ideas about what they wanted to happen. In 1850, Congress passed the Compromise of 1850. This compromise was supposed to keep both the North and the South happy. California was let into the United States as a free state. Selling

A **compromise** is when each side gives up a little and finds a way to meet in the middle.

slaves was outlawed in Washington, D.C. (But people could still own slaves.) And, to make the South happy, the Fugitive Slave Act was passed.

The Fugitive Slave Act said it was against the law to help runaway slaves escape. Anybody who found a runaway slave anywhere in the United States was supposed to capture her. Policemen and other officials got paid more if they helped capture slaves. Runaway slaves were not allowed to speak for themselves in court.

Abolitionists thought the Fugitive Slave Act was horrible. The Underground Railroad

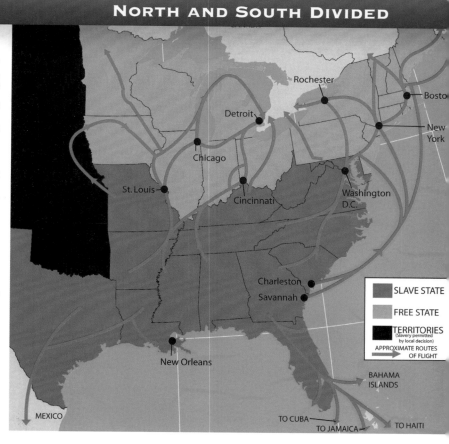

Map of the Underground Railroad

worked harder than ever to rescue people from slavery. In Massachusetts, the government made a law saying it was illegal to **enforce** the new act. Some people were so angry about the act that mobs attacked slave catchers. Then they rescued the runaways.

Enforce means to make sure that a law is obeyed.

People in the South were furious about the North's reaction to the Fugitive Slave Act. The act had been the only thing the South had really liked about the Compromise of 1850. Now the North was ignoring it.

Another argument between the North and the South was where to put a railway across North America. People had been talking for a while about building a railway across the continent. Those in the South thought the railway should be built across the South. Those in the North thought it should take a more northern route, through Nebraska.

In 1854, Senator Stephen Douglas from Illinois started working to have the railway start in Chicago. This would mean it would take the northern route through Nebraska. Douglas hoped people in Illinois would like this idea and vote for him again. He also hoped a northern route for the railway would make him a lot of money. He owned land in the area. He also owned **stock** in the railway.

To get the South to agree to a northern railway route, Douglas suggested the Kansas-Nebraska Act. Nebraska was a large area at that time. The Kansas-Nebraska Act would divide it into two states, Kansas and Nebraska. Each state would be allowed to decide for itself whether it would join the country as a free or a slave state. The problem was that this idea went against the Missouri Compromise. Both Nebraska and Kansas were north of Missouri's southern border. That meant they were both supposed to join the country as free states.

Douglas started working to get rid of the Missouri Compromise. He wanted the South to agree to the Kansas-Nebraska Act. Douglas didn't really care about slavery. He did

If someone owns **stock**, they own a share in a company. This means that when the company makes money, they do too.

STATES' RIGHTS— OR THE NATION'S POWER?

Right at the beginning of the United States, Americans split into two groups. One side wanted a strong government at the center of the United States. The other side worried about giving the nation's central government too much power. They wanted to keep more power for the states. This meant that each state should have the right to decide for themselves about slavery. The nation's central government should stay out of it.

The United States settled the slavery issue more than a hundred years ago. But Americans still argue over states' rights. Should states be able to make their own laws about things like same-sex marriage, the environment, and abortion? Or should the nation's central government be able to pass laws for the entire country? People don't agree.

What do you think?

feel strongly about states' rights, though. He thought each state should be able to decide for itself whether it would be free or slave. He thought the Missouri Compromise took away this right. He had no problem with getting rid of it.

In May of 1854, Congress got rid of the Missouri Compromise. Instead, it passed the Kansas-Nebraska Act. Immediately, groups of abolitionists started moving to Kansas. People in favor of slavery came, too. Each wanted to make sure they could push the vote to be what they wanted it to be.

Over the next couple of years, life in Kansas got ugly. People fought constantly over slavery. Some people were killed. Towns were burned. Kansas got the nickname "Bloody Kansas."

In May of 1856, Massachusetts Senator Charles Sumner gave a speech about the situation. He called it "The Crime Against Kansas." He blamed South Carolina Senator Andrew Butler for trying to force Kansas into becoming a slave state. Sumner was very excited during his speech. He hated slavery. He hated seeing the mess Kansas had become. He said Butler was a liar. He said Butler was slavery's servant.

Butler wasn't there the day Sumner made his speech. His nephew Preston Brooks was, though. Brooks was very offended by what Sumner had said about his uncle. Two days later, Brooks walked up to Sumner in the Senate chamber. Then he hit him in the head with his walking stick. Sumner was knocked unconscious. Several other congressmen were finally able to pull Brooks away. Sumner was so badly hurt he had to spend the next several years recovering in Europe.

Northerners were horrified. Southerners seemed happy about what Brooks had done. Brooks resigned after the attack. But his actions were so popular that people immediately reelected him.

Brooks became a symbol for both the North and the South. People in the South saw him as symbol of their pride. They liked him for not backing down. They were happy he hadn't just accepted the North's insults. People in the North, however, saw Brooks as the image of Southern cruelty. If a Southern gentleman would attack someone in public, what would he do in private? And what would he do to his slaves? The fact that so many Southerners supported Brooks made it worse. People in the North wondered if all Southerners were so cruel. Northerners started to wonder what should be done.

Depiction of Preston Brooks attacking Senator Sumner.

Abraham Lincoln

Chapter Three
THE SOUTH DROPS OUT OF THE UNITED STATES

Before 1858, not many people had heard of Abraham Lincoln. He was best known in his home state of Illinois for being an honest lawyer. For a while, he served as a **politician**, too. Then he quit politics and focused on the law.

When the Kansas-Nebraska Act was passed in 1854, though, Lincoln was upset. He thought the act was a terrible idea. In 1856, he joined the new Republican Party. People from different political parties had formed the Republican Party. Their main goal was to stop slavery from spreading.

In 1858, Lincoln ran against Stephen Douglas in the Illinois Senate race. Douglas had written the Kansas-Nebraska Act. In the fall of 1858, Lincoln and Douglas held a series of **debates**. For two months, they met seven times to debate. Mostly, the debates focused on the spread of slavery. Douglas argued that the country could have both slave states and free states. Lincoln said that the country couldn't go on with both forever. He didn't

A **politician** is someone who is a leader in the government, either at the town, state, or national level.

Debates are discussions or arguments.

For Electors of President and Vice President of the United States,

HORACE GREELEY.   PRESTON KING.

FOR PRESIDENT OF THE UNITED STATES,

ABRAHAM LINCOLN

FOR VICE PRESIDENT OF THE UNITED STATES,

ANDREW JOHNSON.

FOR GOVERNOR,

REUBEN E. FENTON

FOR LIEUTENANT GOVERNOR,

THOMAS G. ALVORD.

For Canal Commissioner,   For Inspector of State Prisons,

FRANKLIN A. ALBERGER. | DAVID P. FORREST

FOR SHERIFF OF THE CITY AND COUNTY OF NEW YORK

JOHN W. FARMER.

FOR DISTRICT ATTORNEY   For Clerk of the City and County of New-York

WM. T. B. MILLIKEN. | JAMES M. THOMPSON.

FOR CORONERS,

LOUIS NAUMANN.   EDWARD COLLIN.   JAMES W. RANNEY.   ALEXANDER WILDER

FOR CITY JUDGE   FOR SUPERVISOR

Orlando L. Stewart | Andreas Willman.

SIMEON DRAPER, Prest. Union Gen. Com.   HARVEY B. WOODS, Sec. U. G. C.   R. C. HAWKINS, the El. Com. U. G. C.

think the country would split up, though. Instead, he thought the United States would have to decide whether all states would be slave or free.

Lincoln lost the Senate election to Douglas. But people across the country now knew who he was. In 1860, the Republican Party chose Lincoln as their **candidate** for President.

The new Republican Party was fairly popular in the North. In the South, though, people didn't want anything to do with the Republicans. The Republicans' wanted to stop the spread of slavery. This was the opposite of what the South wanted.

Four candidates ran for President in the election of 1860. Lincoln won all the free states except New Jersey. He didn't win any of the Southern states. In many Southern states, he wasn't even listed on the ballot. Most of the free states had higher populations than the slave states, though. That meant that Lincoln got more votes from those states.

Before the election, South Carolina had said it would drop out of the United States if Lincoln won. When Lincoln did win, they saw it as a sign that the North wasn't interested in what was good for the South. South Carolina held a vote of

A **candidate** is someone who runs in an election for an office.

their own. They voted on whether or not to leave the United States. The result was **unanimous**—South Carolina would drop out of the country!

Over the next two months, other Southern states followed South Carolina. Mississippi, Florida, Alabama, Georgia, Louisiana, and Texas all voted to drop out of the Union too. In February of 1861, leaders from these states met together. They formed the Confederate States of America. Jefferson Davis, a senator from Mississippi, would be their president.

The Confederacy didn't think the North would try to stop them from dropping out. They thought they were doing the same thing the first thirteen colonies had done when they broke away from Britain. The South also knew the North depended on trade with the South. They didn't think the North would risk its source of money by going to war. War was expensive, after all.

Abraham Lincoln did not become President until a month after the Confederacy had formed. In the meantime, James Buchanan was still President. Buchanan didn't do anything to stop the Southern states from leaving the Union. He didn't think the South was legally allowed to leave the Union like they had. But he didn't think he had any legal right to stop them, either. He didn't think **civil war** was allowed by the **Constitution**.

Lincoln didn't want war, either. When he became President, he told the Confederacy that he wanted the Union to stay together. He also said that the United States wouldn't start a war with the Confederacy. He knew war was a possibility, though. He told the Confederacy the Union wouldn't attack them. The only way a war would happen would be if the Confederacy made the first move.

When something is **unanimous**, that means that absolutely everyone agrees.

Civil war is when a country splits into two sides and fights against each other.

The **Constitution** is the United States' most important set of laws.

Within the Confederacy, two forts had stayed loyal to the United States. One of these, Fort Sumter, was located in the Charleston Harbor. Fort Sumter didn't have enough supplies. When Lincoln discovered this, he sent a message to the Confederacy. He told them he was sending supplies to the fort. He wouldn't send more men, though. He wanted to make sure the Confederacy knew he wasn't trying to attack them.

The Confederacy didn't trust the Union, though. They worried the Union really were trying to attack through Fort Sumter. They quickly moved to take over the fort.

When Fort Sumter's commander refused to surrender, South Carolina attacked the fort. On April 12, 1861, the Union forces surrendered. South Carolina took over Fort Sumter.

The battle of Fort Sumter was the beginning of the Civil War. With that attack, people in the North started calling for war.

Earlier, some of the Southern states hadn't chosen to drop out of the Union. Now they had a choice. They had to decide whether to join the Union or the Confederacy in the war. Virginia, Arkansas, and Tennessee all chose to leave the Union as well. Part of Virginia didn't want to leave, though. This part broke off and became West Virginia.

Delaware, Missouri, Kentucky, and Maryland were all slave states. They bordered on free states, though. Lincoln convinced them not to drop out of the Union. He told them that the war was not about getting rid of slavery. Instead, it was about keeping the country together. And this was true. Even though the outcome of the war would be different from what the slave states hoped.

A sergeant restoring the Stars and Stripes to the ramparts of Fort Sumter before the final fall of the fort to the Confederates.

Chapter Four
THE CIVIL WAR

When the Civil War began, nobody thought it would last long. People in the North thought they could quickly beat the Confederacy. They thought the whole mess would soon be over.

On July 21, 1861, the First Battle of Bull Run took place. (It is also sometimes called the First Battle of Manassas.) The Union Army marched out from Washington, D.C., to attack the Confederate Army. They thought beating the Confederates would be easy. Congressmen brought their families to watch the battle and eat a picnic lunch. They believed it would probably be the only battle in the war. They didn't want to miss it.

Instead of an easy victory, though, the fighting went on for hours. The Union forces weren't very experienced. But they had expected the Confederates to be even worse. Many of the officers on both sides had never fought before. However, the South had Stonewall Jackson.

Thomas Jackson wasn't very well known at that point. He had fought in the Mexican War. He had also been an unpopular teacher at the Virginia Military Institute. With the Battle of Bull Run, though, Jackson became famous. Many soldiers panicked and ran away. Jackson and his men, though, refused to back down. It was in this battle that Jackson earned his nickname "Stonewall." After Bull Run, Stonewall Jackson became one of the most important leaders of the Confederate forces.

People came to watch the Union army at the Battle of Bull Run as though it were a a parade.

The First Battle of Bull Run changed the way the North thought about the war. They had expected to defeat the Confederacy quickly. Instead, their soldiers scattered and panicked. The families who had come to watch also panicked. The roads were blocked with their carriages, as they tried to flee back to Washington. They got in the way of the Army as it tried to retreat. The Union had nearly 3,000 casualties. Most of those were wounded, captured, or missing, while 460 were killed. The Confederacy had nearly 2,000 casualties.

The Civil War was a terrible war. Families were turned against each other. Sometimes brothers fought against each other on different sides. The Civil War was also an example of a "total war." In a total war, each side uses all its resources to destroy the other side's ability to fight. The Civil War was long and expensive. The winner was partly decided by which side had the most money and resources.

The Union and the Confederacy each had different advantages. The Union had better ways to make money. They had farms that grew food. They also had factories. They could make the things they needed for the war.

The Confederacy depended mainly on cotton to make its money. Britain bought a lot of cotton from the South. The Confederacy hoped Britain would support them in the war.

Confederate flag and weapons

Britain didn't support them, though. Most people in Britain thought slavery was evil. They weren't going to help the Confederacy fight to keep their slaves. Britain also had a lot of cotton in warehouses. It wasn't going to need more cotton for a while.

The Confederacy had better officers than the Union, though. One of their generals was Robert E. Lee. Lee had been an officer in the United States Army. He was serving in Texas when he got the news that the South had split away from the Union. At the same time, he received orders to go back to Washington. He was going to be asked to fight for the Union. Lee was from Virginia. He didn't want to fight against his own people. Instead, he resigned from the U.S. Army. When the Confederacy asked him to lead the Virginian forces, he agreed. He didn't want to fight at all. But he was loyal to Virginia. He didn't think of saying no.

Robert E. Lee was an experienced officer. Stonewall Jackson was a skilled general, too. The Union, on the other hand, had a lot of officers who didn't know what they were doing. In 1864, three years after the war began, the Union finally found Ulysses S. Grant. Grant was the best officer the Union had.

For the first year of the war, Lincoln argued that he was only fighting to keep the United States together. He did not want to talk about slavery at first. The northern-most slave states—Maryland, Delaware, Kentucky, and Missouri—had not joined the Confederacy. Lincoln was afraid if he said he wanted to end slavery, those states would drop out too. Finally, in September 1862, the Union won its first major battle. Lincoln now felt he could talk about slavery safely. On September 22, 1862, he issued the Emancipation Proclamation. The **Emancipation Proclamation** freed all the slaves in the Confederacy.

Emancipation means the act of setting free.

A **proclamation** is an official statement.

Emancipation Proclamation

After the Emancipation Proclamation, the war changed. The Confederacy knew things could never go back to the way they had been. The Union now had a new reason for fighting, though. Union soldiers were now fighting to free the slaves. The Emancipation Proclamation also made other countries want to help the Union. Countries like Britain, that believed slavery was wrong, now backed the Union's fight.

The most famous battle of the Civil War was the Battle of Gettysburg. It took place in July of 1863. Gettysburg was a huge battle. It was also the turning point of the Civil War.

General Robert E. Lee liked to leave the small decisions during a battle to his commanding officers. This worked well when Stonewall Jackson was taking charge. But

Jackson had died two months earlier. Several of Lee's new commanders were working with him for the first time.

The battle had been going on for two days when Lee ordered an attack on the Union forces. The attack became known as Pickett's Charge. It was named for General George Pickett, one of the Confederate Generals who led the charge. Pickett's Charge failed. The Confederate forces moved across three-quarters of a mile of open ground toward the Union forces. Although some of them reached the Union forces, many were killed or hurt. Those who reached the Union line were quickly pushed back.

Gettysburg, Pennsylvania

The Battle of Gettysburg scared the Confederacy. Before this, they really thought they would win the war. Gettysburg, in Southern Pennsylvania, marked the furthest north the Confederacy reached.

In March 1864, President Lincoln put General Ulysses S. Grant in charge of all the Union forces. Grant gave General William T. Sherman the job of capturing Georgia. Sherman hated war. He thought it was necessary, though. He fought to win. He tried to win quickly, too. Sherman's March to the Sea destroyed everything—but it was successful. Sherman and his forces marched through Georgia, burning houses, fields, and whole towns. He even burned Atlanta. He wanted to destroy the Confederacy's resources. He also wanted to break them. In December 1864, Sherman reached Savannah and captured it.

While Sherman fought in Georgia, Grant fought Robert E. Lee in Virginia. The Confederacy was running out of money. They were tired. In April 1865, Lee gave up Richmond, Virginia, to the Union. He and his men went back to the village of Appomattox Courthouse. There, Grant's forces surrounded them. On April 9, 1865, Lee gave up.

After Lee gave up, the war was basically over. The rest of the Confederacy's forces soon surrendered, too.

Lee and Grant signing a peace agreement between the North and South.

John Wilkes Booth fleeing Ford's Theatre after shooting Lincoln.

Chapter Five
RECONSTRUCTION

On April 14, 1865, President Abraham Lincoln went to see a play. Robert E. Lee had surrendered five days earlier. The people in Washington, D.C., were happy and excited.

Lincoln sat in a box overlooking the stage. While he, his wife, and his friends watched the play, a man snuck up behind him. The man was John Wilkes Booth. Booth hated Lincoln. He was angry the Union had won the Civil War. He was so angry he wanted to kill Lincoln. So he walked up behind Lincoln at the theater—and he shot him in the head.

People carried Lincoln across the road. They tried to save his life. But it was no good. He died the next morning.

John Wilkes Booth ran away after shooting Lincoln. Twelve days later, soldiers found him. He was shot and killed as they tried to capture him.

Booth hadn't just wanted to kill Lincoln, though. He'd also sent men to kill Vice President Andrew Johnson and Secretary of State William Seward. He hoped that killing the three most important men in Washington would turn the government into a big mess. He hoped the Confederacy would be able to take advantage of that mess. He thought maybe the Confederacy could rise up again after all.

The man who was supposed to take Andrew Johnson's life didn't try to kill him, though. He hadn't really liked the plan. William Seward was attacked and he was hurt, but he lived.

Booth's plan didn't work as well as he had hoped. Lincoln's death changed the country, though. For one thing, people in the North blamed the South. This made them even angrier with the South.

After Lincoln's death, Vice President Andrew Johnson became President. Johnson had some good points, but he was not the best person to deal with putting the country back together.

Even before the war had ended, Lincoln had made a plan for bringing the country together again. He knew it would be hard work. Under Lincoln's plan, the Southern states would be brought back into the Union after they had agreed to certain things. Each state needed at least 10 percent of its voters to agree to free their slaves. Congress worried that Lincoln's conditions weren't strict enough. They thought more voters should have to agree before a state could be let back into the Union.

The Emancipation Proclamation had freed hundreds of thousands of slaves. One of the biggest challenges of Reconstruction was helping these people move from slavery to freedom. The entire way Southerners lived needed to change.

John Wilkes Booth

The Freedman's Bureau was set up to help with this change. The Freedman's Bureau helped people who had been slaves get work and education. They also helped with emergency needs like food, shelter, and clothing.

Many white people in the South had trouble getting used to the idea of free black people. Some people tricked freed slaves into signing work **contracts**. These contracts basically made them slaves again. Groups like the Freedman's Bureau tried to keep things like that from happening.

After they had rejoined the Union, Southern states made the "Black Codes." These were laws that tried to control blacks' freedom. The laws took away many of blacks' rights. They were slightly different in different states. In Mississippi, for example, if a black person didn't work hard enough, he had to work for a year without pay. In South Carolina, black farm workers had to work from sunrise to sunset six days a week. They also had to call their employers "masters."

People in the North were furious about the Black Codes. They had fought a war to end slavery. Now it seemed the South was trying to continue slavery anyway. In 1866, Congress outlawed the Black Codes. They also passed a Civil Rights Act. The Act gave **citizenship** to everyone who had been born in the United States. It didn't matter what race a person was or if he ever had been a slave.

In 1867, Congress passed the first of the Reconstruction Acts. These acts gave control of the Southern states to U.S. government. The South was divided into five districts. Union generals ruled the districts. Union soldiers kept order. Another part of the acts gave

A **contract** is a written legal agreement.

Citizenship means all the rights that go along with being a member of a country or state.

all men in the United States the right to vote. This meant black men as well as white men. Congress talked about giving women the right to vote as well, but they decided not to.

The South was a mess for a long time after the Civil War. Life had changed completely. People had trouble getting used to the changes. Slave owners had to get used to life without slaves. Freed slaves worked to find their place. Some black men were excited about their new freedoms. During the Reconstruction years, many black men became mayors, congressmen, senators, and sheriffs.

As the Southern states gradually took their place within the Union again, they were set up with Republican governments. Before the Civil War and Reconstruction, the Republican Party hadn't existed in the South. The Republicans were against slavery. The Southern Democrats at this time had been for slavery. Now, many Northerners moved South to join the state Republican parties. They arrived carrying all their belongings in suitcases made of carpet. The Southerners called them carpetbaggers. They did not like the carpetbaggers. They saw them as men who were trying to use the situation. The carpetbaggers didn't usually care much about the South. They just wanted power.

Some white Southerners were also very angry about black people getting political power. Some of them

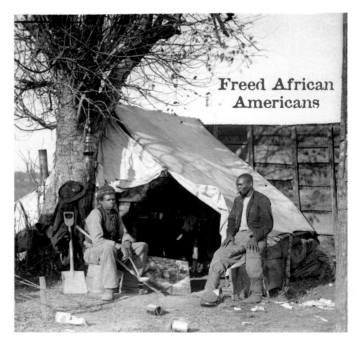

Freed African Americans

were so angry they formed secret groups like the Ku Klux Klan. The Ku Klux Klan (also called the KKK) was a group that thought black people weren't as good as white people. They tried to scare black people into leaving their leadership positions or their jobs. If that didn't work, sometimes the KKK beat them up or even killed them.

In 1868, Ulysses S. Grant became President of the United States. He had been a very popular Union general during the Civil War. He did not make as good a President as he had a general, though. He was not a bad man, but he didn't know how to deal with other people who were bad. Sometimes, he didn't notice when people around lied or did bad things. Even after he knew, though, he didn't like to deal with it. While Grant was President, many of the leaders in the United States lied. They gave money or favors to people who agreed to help them. The country was still a mess from the Civil War.

In 1876, Rutherford B. Hayes ran against Samuel J. Tilden for President. The number of votes for both sides was very close together. Neither Hayes' Republicans nor Tilden's Democrats could agree who had won. The arguments went on for months. Finally, on March 2, 1877, two days before the **inauguration**, they agreed to name Hayes as President. In exchange, Hayes would take the rest of U.S. troops out of the South.

The Civil War and the years before and after it had been a rough time for the United States. Things had changed a lot. The changes had freed the slaves and made them citizens. All men now had the right to vote. But life was still hard for black people in the South. When the U.S. troops left the South, many Southern states passed new laws that cut back on black's freedom. It would be another hundred years before the Civil Rights movement gave blacks equal rights in the United States.

An **inauguration** is when an official (like the President) is sworn into office and begins to serve his or her term in office.

FIND OUT MORE

In Books

Bolotin, Norman. *Civil War: A to Z.* New York: Dutton Children's Books, 2002.

Corrick, James A. *Life Among the Soldiers and Cavalry.* San Diego: Lucent, 2000.

Damon, Duane. *Growing Up in the Civil War.* Minneapolis: Lerner, 2003.

Fradin, Dennis Brindell. *Bound for the North Star: True Stories of Fugitive Slaves.* New York: Clarion, 2000.

McPherson, James. *Fields of Fury: The American Civil War.* New York: Atheneum, 2002.

Stanchack, John. *Eyewitness: Civil War.* New York: DK, 2000.

On the Internet

Abraham Lincoln
members.aol.com/RVSNorton/Lincoln2.html

The Civil War
americancivilwar.com
www.civilwar.com
www.swcivilwar.com

A Civil War Timeline
www.historyplace.com/civilwar

Reconstruction
americanhistory.about.com/cs/reconstruction

Slavery
www.digitalhistory.uh.edu/black_voices/blackvoices.cfm

INDEX

ABOUT THE AUTHOR AND THE CONSULTANT

Wesley Windsor lived much of his life in Canada's far north, where he grew up with an appreciation of wild places. He received a master's degree in English literature from the University of Rochester, and he has previously written many fiction books for children under another name. As the parent of two children, he hopes to raise them with a love of nature and a respect for history.

Dr. Jack N. Rakove is a professor of history and American studies at Stanford University, where he is director of American studies. The winner of the 1997 Pulitzer Prize in history, Dr. Rakove is the author of *The Unfinished Election of 2000*, *Constitutional Culture and Democratic Rule*, and *James Madison and the Creation of the American Republic*. He is also the president of the Society for the History of the Early American Republic.